MW01175158

Table of Contents

18. Smokey Bacon Meatballs
19. Chicken Bacon Sauté
20. Pepperoni Meatballs
21. Parmesan Crusted Chicken Thighs
22. Garlic Butter Chicken
23. Garlic Bacon Wrapped Chicken Bites
24. Pinchos de Pollo (Kebabs)
25. Carnivore Waffles
26. Carnivore French Fries
27. Grilled Chicken Drumsticks with Garlic Marinade

Fish and Seafood
28. Salmon and Cream Cheese Bites
29. Baked Fish Fillets
30. Salmon Cakes
31. Grilled Split Lobster
32. Fish Bone Broth
33. Garlic Butter Shrimp
34. Grilled Shrimp
35. Garlic Ghee Pan-Fried Cod

Organ Meat
36. Pan-Seared Beef Tongue
37. Moroccan Liver Kebabs
38. Carnivore Quiche (Organ Meat Pie)
39. Easy Beef Heart
40. Carnivore Cake
41. Easy Beef Kidney Bites
42. Beef and Chicken Liver Burgers
43. Chicken Hearts
44. Roasted Bone Marrow
45. Chicken Liver Pate

CONCLUSION

Introduction

I want to first thank you for choosing the *The Carnivore Diet Cookbook*.

The carnivore diet might be a relatively new concept for you, but it's based on an eating protocol that dates back to our cavemen ancestors. The carnivore diet, as the name suggests, is predominantly meat-based. You are free to consume all animal foods such as meats, seafood, eggs, and some dairy products in limited quantities. As long as you stick to this protocol, you can obtain the different benefits this diet offers. If you want to lose weight, improve your overall health, feel energetic, and strengthen your muscles, this diet will help.

In this book, you'll discover several easy to cook carnivore diet-based recipes. All the recipes are not only easy to understand, but the instructions are simple. All you need to do is stock your pantry with the advised carnivore-friendly ingredients, pick a recipe, and start cooking.

Once you get used to the recipes, you will realize, cooking this way is not much different from how you cook now, and the meals are delicious! Forget about eating bland food for the sake of a diet. Tantalize your taste buds with the assorted recipes you will discover in these pages. Starting a new diet isn't always easy, and to make things easier, we will create a 2-week meal plan using only the recipes found here. You can tweak the meal plan according to your preferences, of course.

Chapter 1: What You Need to Know

What is the Carnivore Diet?

The carnivore diet's premise is that humans have survived and thrived on a diet predominantly consisting of meat and seafood. It is very similar to the diet followed by our ancestors. There is widespread belief that the increasing rate of chronic illnesses plaguing society today is associated with diets high in fat, sugar, and carbs. Before agriculture was introduced, humans lived on animal meat and grains considerably rich in protein and low on carbohydrates.

To maintain function of the major organs and to actively heal itself, the human body requires a lot of energy. When you consume a diet rich in plant-based foods, most of the energy available is often used to convert all these foods into usable nutrients. Plant-based foods are generally low in vital nutrients such as omega-3 fatty acids, vitamin A, vitamin D, vitamin K2, zinc, B-12, and iodine. Consuming animal meats is the simplest way to make up for these essential nutrients.

Anything derived from an animal is perfectly suitable here. It's a new diet compared to others that span decades, but the idea isn't new at all. Dr. Sean Baker, a famous orthopedic surgeon and athlete is accredited with creating this diet. His personal dietary experiences, coupled with a refreshing take on the ideal human diet, have successfully revolutionized nutrition.

Think about this for a moment: Have humans always predominantly consumed plants? Our cavemen ancestors were hunters and gatherers. They depended on animals to sustain them and survive. The human diet has undergone a drastic change in the last 10,000 years after the invention of agriculture. With humans now able to grow and harvest different types of grains and legumes, their diets also changed. In that time, we have managed to rewrite 2 million years of evolution. With such a drastic change, it is no surprise humanity now suffers more frequently from chronic illness and disease; evolution never got a chance to catch up.

Humans have become smaller in stature in this time frame and have seen a decrease in brain size. A diet that primarily consists of grains and sugars is the reason various illnesses such as cancer, obesity, diabetes, and osteoporosis. It is also a reason for the significant increase in the risk for cardiovascular disease, inflammatory conditions, and skin issues. Human genes developed and evolved before agriculture came into the picture. If our caveman ancestors not only survived but thrived on this diet, why can't you?

It's a popular belief that you are free to consume whatever you want as long as you exercise. Well, even Sean Baker agreed. However, all this started to change once he entered his 40s. During this period, Baker began to experience problems, such as metabolic syndrome, joint troubles, and back pain associated with his athletic career's usual wear and tear. His body was not burning calories like it once did, and he was unable to eat all that he wanted. During this period, he concentrated on the origins of the human diet and explored this idea further. After a lot of research, he stumbled upon the secret that consuming higher amounts of meat is vital for staying fit and maintaining a healthy weight.

All sorts of animal products can be safely included in this diet. Fish, meat, and eggs are the primary source of food and dairy products. Even though dairy is derived from an animal source, it contains lactose, a form of carbs. This diet is low in carbs, and instead, increases the intake of healthy proteins and fats. You can include beef, turkey, lamb, salmon, white fish, eggs, pork, chicken, bone marrow, organ meats, hard cheeses, lard, and some cream. Just because it's a meat-based diet doesn't mean you should default to excessive processed and prepackaged meats. Limit your intake of any processed meats such as salami, sausages, and bacon if you want to stick to this diet's protocols.

Benefits of the Carnivore Diet

As mentioned, humans were designed to be meat-eaters. Therefore, not eating meat can cause severe problems. In this section, let's look at the many benefits of the carnivore diet.

Increased Energy Levels

Carbs and sugars are quickly burned by the body to provide energy. It can make you feel energetic immediately, but a quick energy crash will follow. This instability can harm your body's overall functioning. The brain uses orexin cells to determine energy levels. If these cells are active, you feel instantly energized. Consuming amino acids is the best way to stimulate these cells. Therefore, the carnivore diet will enhance your overall energy levels. It is also rich in iron. Did you know that iron deficiency or anemia reduces energy? Say goodbye to these problems with the carnivore diet.

Rich in Nutrients

The carnivore diet encourages the consumption of foods rich in proteins, vital vitamins, and minerals. Proteins are the source of helpful amino acids that act as building blocks for different body molecules. Amino acids help synthesize new proteins, replace red blood cells, manufacture antibodies, and develop muscle. There are approximately 20 types of amino acids present in proteins, and the body manufactures nearly half of them. However, essential amino acids are derived from dietary sources. Any deficiency in these essential amino acids causes protein loss.

Not just protein, meats are also rich in important minerals and essential vitamins. Various minerals are required for the overall functioning of cells and different tissues in the body. Meats are rich in iron, zinc, phosphorus, and sulfur. The body requires oxygen for its functioning, and iron is needed for its transportation. Zinc helps strengthen the immune system while phosphorus strengthens the muscles and enhances the essential amino acids' functioning. The most important vitamin provided by meat is B-12. Vitamin B-12 is quintessential for maintaining and improving the health of the nervous and circulatory systems. It assists in protein synthesis and metabolism and improves your body's overall functioning.

Good for Neurotransmitters

Lack of meat protein creates imbalances in neurotransmitters that are ideal for supplying amino acids throughout the body. Different chemical messengers known as neurotransmitters govern your body's mental, physical, and cognitive functioning. It also regulates other vital functions such as sleep cycle, emotional state, and weight. Any imbalance in these essential neurotransmitters causes hyperactivity, depression, or even anxiety.

Stabilization of Blood Sugar Levels

The dietary fats and helpful proteins present in meats help regulate and stabilize blood sugar levels. Type-2 diabetes is a harmful condition, and a risk factor for chronic illness. Once your blood sugar levels are stabilized, your energy levels improve. It also reduces cravings for unhealthy junk foods while promoting the feeling of satiety. Most cravings for junk foods rich in carbs and sugars are due to fluctuations in the blood sugar levels. Eating meat neutralizes this problem, and naturally reduces your intake of unhealthy foods.

Promotes Muscle Growth

As mentioned earlier, your body needs plenty of protein to build and develop its muscles. For building muscles, you need to exercise. However, irrespective of how much exercise you cannot attain this goal without proper nutrition. While you exercise to build muscle, your body requires plenty of protein for recovery. This is known as "gains" of exercise. If your body doesn't get the necessary nutrients to repair and recover itself, you cannot obtain these games from exercise. The best source of dietary protein is meat.

Meats promote muscle development while encouraging your body to burn fats. The thermogenic effect of meat is high due to its protein content. The body burns about 30% of the calories you consume from meat during digestion. However, your body uses only about 6-8% of its energy to digest and absorb carbs or sugars. By increasing your body's ability to burn fats and building muscles, attaining your fitness goals becomes easier.

What to Avoid?

You can consume all types of meats, seafood, low-carb condiments, spices, herbs, and other animal foods such as organ meats, eggs, bone marrow, and dairy. The list of foods you should avoid on this diet is pretty straightforward.

Any food, which is not obtained from animals, is excluded from this diet. You need to avoid fruits, vegetables, nuts and seeds, legumes, sugars, and dairy products with high lactose content. You are also not allowed to consume any beverages except water. If you want to improve your overall health and lose weight, stay away from alcohol. The same rule applies to all prepackaged foods rich in carbs, sugars, and unhealthy processed ingredients.

Chapter 2: Let's Get Cooking:

Red Meat

1. Breakfast Sausage

Preparation time: 15 minutes Cooking time: 15 minutes Number of servings: 12

Ingredients:

- 1 ½ pound ground pork or beef or a mixture of both
- ¾ teaspoon dried parsley
- ½ teaspoon pepper
- ¼ teaspoon crushed red pepper
- 2 tablespoons bacon fat or ghee or lard
- 1 ½ teaspoon salt or to taste
- ½ teaspoon dried sage
- ¼ teaspoon fennel seeds
- ½ teaspoon ground coriander

Directions:

1. Add meat, salt, dried herbs, and spices into a bowl and mix well.
2. Make 12 patties and pan-fry them with bacon fat. Cook until it becomes brown.
3. Turn the patties over and cook well on both sides.
4. Remove the patties and place them on paper towels.

5. Cook the remaining sausages similarly.

6. You can freeze these sausage patties. For this, once the sausages are cooled, transfer onto a baking sheet and freeze until firm.

7. Remove the frozen sausages from the baking sheet and place them in freezer-safe bags. You can freeze the sausages for up to 6 months.

8. If you do not want to freeze them, place the sausages in an airtight container in the refrigerator. Use within 5 – 6 days.

Nutritional values per serving:

9. Calories – 172 | Fat – 14 g | Carbohydrate – 0 g | Protein – 9 g

2.Carnivore Breakfast Sandwich

Preparation time: 5 minutesCooking time: 5 minutesNumber of servings: 2

Ingredients:

- 4 sausage patties (if necessary, refer to the previous recipe)
- 2 slices cheddar cheese (2 ounces)
- 2 eggs
- 2 teaspoons butter or bacon fat
- Salt and pepper to taste

Directions:

1. Flatten the patties to about ½ inch thickness.
2. Place a skillet over medium flame. Add 1-teaspoon butter. Once the butter melts, place patties in the pan.
3. Cook until brown on the underside. Flip the patties over and cook well on the other side too.
4. Remove the patties from the pan using a slotted spoon and set aside on layers of paper towels to drain.
5. Add another teaspoon of butter into the pan. Once butter melts, crack the eggs in the pan. Cook eggs sunny side up. Season the eggs with salt and pepper.

6. To make the sandwich: Place 2 patties on a plate and place an egg on each patty followed by a slice of cheese. Complete the sandwich by covering with the remaining patties and serve.

Nutritional values per serving:

Calories – 448 | Fat – 36 g | Carbohydrate – 1 g | Protein – 33 g

3.Breakfast Casserole with Bacon and Sausage

Preparation time: 20 minutesCooking time: 30 minutesNumber of servings: 6 (4.3 oz each)

Ingredients:

- 6 eggs
- 6 slices bacon, cooked crumbled
- 1 cup grated parmesan cheese
- ¾ pound sausages
- 6 tablespoons heavy cream
- 1 teaspoon hot sauce like Frank's or to taste
- Seasonings of your choice

Directions:

1. Add a little animal fat into a casserole dish and grease it well.
2. Make sure that your oven is preheated to 350° F.
3. Place a skillet with sausage over medium flame. Cook until brown. You have to crumble it as it cooks. Turn off the heat.
4. Add bacon and mix well. Spread the meat mixture in the casserole.
5. Sprinkle ½ cup cheese over the meat.
6. Blend eggs, cream, hot sauce, and seasonings in a blender until smooth.
7. Drizzle over the meat and cheese layer. Sprinkle remaining cheese on top.

8. Bake the casserole for about 30 minutes or until it is well cooked inside. To check, insert a knife in the casserole dish's center and pull it out immediately. If any particles are on the knife, bake for a few more minutes.

9. Cool for 10–12 minutes and serve.

Nutritional values per serving:

Calories – 388 | Fat – 32 g | Carbohydrate – 1 g | Protein – 22 g

4.Skillet Rib Eye Steaks

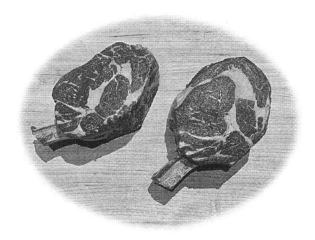

Preparation time: 30 minutesCooking time: 2 – 6 minutesNumber of servings: 4 (4 oz each)

Ingredients:

- 2 bone-in ribeye steaks (1 ¼ – 1 ½ inch thick)
- 4 teaspoons finely chopped fresh rosemary leaves
- 2 tablespoons olive oil
- 2 teaspoons Stone House seasoning or any other seasoning of your choice
- 2 tablespoons unsalted butter

Directions:

1. Sprinkle seasoning all over the steaks. Rub it well into it.
2. Place it on a baking sheet and scatter rosemary leaves over it.
3. Cover the baking sheet with cling wrap and place it in the refrigerator. They will stay fresh for up to 3 days.
4. Remove the baking sheet from the refrigerator 30 minutes before cooking and place it on your countertop.
5. Place a skillet over medium-high heat and allow it to heat. Add oil and butter and wait for the butter to melt.
6. Place steaks in the skillet.

7. For rare: Cook for 2-3 minutes on both sides, so that the steak becomes golden brown on all sides. Baste the steaks with the liquid as it continues to cook.

8. Using a pair of tongs (behind part), press the steak in the center. When it is soft, remove the steak from the pan and place it on a cutting board.

9. For medium: Cook for 4 minutes or until the underside is slightly golden brown. Turn sides once and cook the other side for 4 minutes. Baste the steaks with the cooked liquid as it is cooking.

10. Using a pair of tongs press the steak in the center. If it is slightly more firm, remove the steaks from the pan.

11. For well done: Cook for 5-6 minutes or until the underside is golden brown. Turn sides once and cook the other side for 5-6 minutes. Baste the steaks with the cooked liquid as it is cooking.

12. Using a pair of tongs (behind part), press the steak in the center. If it is very firm, remove the steaks from the pan.

13. When the steaks are cooked as per your liking, remove steaks from the pan and place them on a cutting board.

14. Cover the steak with foil and allow it to rest for 5 minutes.

15. Slice against the grain and serve.

Nutritional values per serving:

Calories – 347 | Fat – 28 g | Carbohydrate – 0 g | Protein – 22 g

5.Scotch Eggs

Preparation time: 10 minutesCooking time: 30 minutesNumber of servings: 3

Ingredients:

- ☐ 3 medium eggs, hardboiled, peeled
- ☐ 1 teaspoon herbs or spices of your choice
- ☐ ¼ teaspoon salt or to taste
- ☐

- ☐ ½ pound ground red meat of your choice
- ☐ Pepper to taste (optional)

Directions:

1. Preheat your oven to 350° F.
2. Dry the eggs by patting with a kitchen towel.
3. Use any preferred spices. A few suggestions are curry powder, mustard, parsley, Italian seasoning, or Old Bay, etc. Preferably use lean meat else the meat covering the egg may come off when the fat melts.
4. Combine meat, seasoning salt, and pepper in a bowl. Divide the mixture into 3 equal portions.
5. Take a portion of meat and flatten it with your palm. Place an egg in the center and enclose the egg with the meat (like a dumpling). Place on a greased baking sheet.
6. Repeat the previous step and make the other scotch eggs.

7. Place the baking sheet in the oven and bake for about 25 to 30 minutes or until golden brown on top.

Nutritional values per serving:

Calories – 169 | Fat – 8.2 g | Carbohydrate – 0.67 g | Protein – 23.1 g

6.Cheesy Meatballs

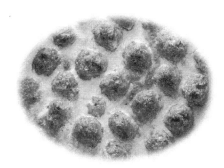

Preparation time: 15 minutesCooking time: About 20 minutesNumber of servings: 3 (4meatballs)

Ingredients:

- ☐ 1-ounce pork rinds
- ☐ 1-pound grass-fed ground beef
- ☐ ½ teaspoon pink sea salt

- ☐ 1 ½ ounce shredded Italian cheese blend
- ☐ 1 large pastured egg
- ☐ ½ tablespoon lard

Directions:

1. Prepare a baking sheet by lining it with parchment paper. Preheat your oven to 350° F.
2. Combine beef, pork rinds, salt, egg, cheese, and lard in a bowl. Make 12 equal portions of the mixture and form into balls. Place the balls on a baking sheet.
3. Bake the meatballs for about 20-30 minutes. Turn the balls around after about 10-12 minutes of baking. When the meatballs are cooked well, the internal temperature in the center of the meatball should be 165° F.
4. You can cook the meatballs in an air fryer if you own one. Turn the balls around a couple of times while cooking in the air fryer.
5. Remove the meatballs from the pan and serve.

Nutritional values per serving:

Calories – 461 | Fat – 32 g | Carbohydrate – 1 g | Protein – 40 g

7.Steak Nuggets

Preparation time: 15 minutesCooking time: 2–3 minutes per batchNumber of servings: 8

Ingredients:

- 2 pounds venison steak or beef steak, chopped into chunks
- Lard, as required, to fry

- 2 large pastured eggs

  Breading
- 1 cup grated parmesan cheese

- 1 teaspoon seasoned salt
- 1 cup pork panko

Directions:

1. Beat eggs in a bowl.
2. Add pork panko, salt, and parmesan into a shallow bowl and stir.
3. First, dunk the steak pieces in egg, one at a time. Shaking off the extra liquid, dredge it in parmesan mixture and place it on a plate.
4. Repeat this process with the remaining steak pieces.
5. Pour enough lard in a deep pan. Place the pan over medium flame and let the lard heat.
6. When the oil is heated to around 325° F, carefully drop a few of the breaded steak pieces in the oil. Turn the steak pieces around a few times so that they are browned uniformly all over.
7. Remove the steak with a slotted spoon and place it on a plate that has been lined with paper towels. Let it drain for a few minutes. Cook the remaining steak pieces similarly (steps 6–7). Serve.

Nutritional values per serving:

Calories – 350 | Fat – 20 g | Carbohydrate – 1 g | Protein – 40 g

8.Grilled Lamb Chops

Preparation time: 20 minutesCooking time: 6 minutesNumber of servings: 4

Ingredients:

- 4 lamb chops (¾ inch thick)
- ½ tablespoon finely chopped fresh rosemary
- Salt to taste
- 1 ½ tablespoon extra-virgin olive oil
- 2 cloves garlic, peeled, minced
- Freshly ground pepper to taste

Directions:

1. Add rosemary, salt, oil, garlic, and pepper into a bowl and mix well.
2. Spread this mixture all over the chops and place in a bowl. Let it marinate for around 15 minutes.
3. In the meantime, set up your grill and preheat it to medium-high. You can also cook it in a grill pan.
4. For rare: Cook for 2-3 minutes or until the underside is light golden brown. Turn sides once and cook the other side for 2-3 minutes.

5. For medium-rare: Cook for 4 minutes or until the underside is slightly golden brown. Turn sides once and cook the other side for 4 minutes.

6. Remove with a slotted spoon and place on a serving platter that has been lined with parchment paper.

7. Serve after resting it for 5 minutes.

Nutritional values per serving:

Calories – 239 | Fat – 16 g | Carbohydrate – 1 g | Protein – 23 g

9.Roasted Leg of Lamb

Preparation time: 15 minutesCooking time: 1 hour and 30 minutesNumber of servings: 6

Ingredients:

- 2 cloves garlic, peeled, sliced
- Salt to taste
- 2 ½ pounds leg of lamb
- Few sprigs fresh rosemary
- Pepper to taste

Directions:

1. Prepare a baking pan by greasing with some fat. Make sure that your oven is preheated to 350° F.
2. Make a few slits all over the lamb. Fill the slits with garlic slices.
3. Sprinkle a generous amount of salt and pepper on the lamb legs.
4. Scatter a few rosemary sprigs in the pan and place the lamb legs over it. Scatter some rosemary sprigs over the legs as well.
5. Roast for about 1 hour and 30 minutes or the way you prefer it cooked. For medium-rare, the internal temperature in the middle of the thickest part of the meat should show 135° F.

Nutritional values per serving:

Calories – 381.8 | Fat – 25.3 g\Carbohydrate – 0.4 g\Protein – 35.8 g

10.Pork Ramen Broth

Preparation time: 20 minutesCooking time: 12 – 15 hoursNumber of servings: 4

Ingredients:

- 1.1 pounds pork bones, without any meat, chopped into large pieces
- 2 ¾ pounds pig trotters, only leg portion, chopped into smaller pieces
- 1 chicken carcass
- 5.3 ounces of pork skin
- 7 ½ quarts water and extra to blanch

Directions:

1. For blanching bones: Take a large pot. Place pig trotters and pork bones in it. Pour enough water to cover the bones.
2. Place the pot over medium flame. Let it come to a boil for about 10 minutes. Remove from heat. Remove the bones and keep it aside.
3. Discard the water and rinse the pot well.
4. Clean the bones of any blood clots and scum with a sharp knife. Make sure to remove all of it.

5. Add 7.5 quarts water into a large pot. Bring to a boil. Add the bones into the pot. Also, add pork skin.

6. Lower heat and let it simmer.

7. Initially, scum will start floating to the top. Remove the scum with a large spoon and discard it. Trim the excess fat as well.

8. Cover the pot with a lid and simmer for about 12- 15 hours. The stock would have reduced in quantity and will be thicker and somewhat cloudy.

9. Remove from heat. When it cools down, strain into a large jar with a wire mesh strainer.

10. Refrigerate for 5–6 days. Unused broth can be frozen.

11. To serve: Heat thoroughly. Add salt and pepper to taste and serve.

Nutritional values per serving:

Calories – 272 | Fat – 15 g | Carbohydrate – 0 g | Protein – 30 g

11.Pan-Fried Pork Tenderloin

Preparation time: 10 minutesCooking time: 20 minutesNumber of servings: 4

Ingredients:

- 2 pounds pork tenderloin, quartered
- Salt and pepper to taste
- 2 tablespoons ghee or lard

Directions:

1. Place a large skillet over medium flame. Add fat and let it melt.
2. Add pork and cook for a few minutes undisturbed. Turn and cook the other sides similarly until the meat's internal temperature in the thickest part shows 145° F.
3. Remove pork from the pan and place it on your cutting board. When cool enough to handle, cut into 1-inch thick slices. Serve.

Nutritional values per serving:

Calories – 330 | Fat – 15 g | Carbohydrate – 0 g | Protein – 47 g

12. Carnivore Baked Eggs

Preparation time: 5 minutesCooking time: 10 minutesNumber of servings: 2

Ingredients:

- ½ tablespoon salted butter
- ½ teaspoon dried parsley
- ¼ teaspoon ground smoked paprika
- 2 large eggs

- 3.5 ounces ground beef
- ½ teaspoon ground cumin
- Salt and pepper to taste
- ¼ cup grated cheddar cheese

Directions:

1. Preheat your oven to 400° F.
2. Add butter into a small ovenproof skillet and place it over a high flame and allow it to melt.
3. Add beef and cook for a minute, stirring all the while.
4. Stir in paprika, salt, pepper, cumin, and parsley. Break the meat as it cooks. Turn off the heat.
5. Lay out the meat mixture evenly, all over the pan. Make 2 holes in the pan. The holes should be big enough for an egg to fit in.
6. Break an egg each in every cavity.

7. Place the skillet into the oven and bake until the eggs are cooked the way you prefer.

8. If you don't have an oven safe skillet, you can use a baking tray instead. Serve hot.

Nutritional values per serving:

Calories – 263 | Fat – 20 g | Carbohydrate – 1.5 g | Protein – 19 g

13.Creamy Garlic Chicken Soup

Preparation time: 10 minutesCooking time: 20 minutesNumber of servings: 8

Ingredients:

- 4 tablespoons butter
- 8 ounces cream cheese, cubed
- 2 cans (14.5 ounces each) chicken broth
- Salt and pepper to taste
- 4 cups cooked, shredded chicken
- 4 tablespoons garlic gusto seasoning or 1
- teaspoon garlic powder
- ½ cup heavy cream

Directions:

1. Place a soup pot over medium flame and melt some butter in it.
2. Once butter melts, stir in the chicken and cook for a couple of minutes.
3. Stir in cream cheese and seasonings. Mix well.
4. Pour broth and cream and stir.

5. Once it boils, reduce the heat and cook for about 5 to 6 minutes.Ladle into soup bowls and serve.

Nutritional values per serving:

Calories – 307 | Fat – 25 g | Carbohydrate – 2 g | Protein – 18 g

14. Chicken Wings

Preparation time: 10 minutesCooking time: 40 – 60 minutesNumber of servings: 4

Ingredients:

- 2 pounds of chicken wings
- ¼ cup freshly grated parmesan cheese
- ¼ teaspoon pepper

- ½ teaspoon salt
- ½ tablespoon minced fresh parsley of ½ teaspoon dried parsley
- 2 –3 tablespoons grass-fed butter

Directions:

1. Prepare a baking sheet by lining it with parchment paper. Preheat the oven to 350° F.
2. Add butter into a microwave-safe shallow bowl. Cook on high for 15 – 20 seconds or until butter just melts.
3. Place salt, pepper, parsley, and parmesan cheese in a bowl and stir well.
4. Dunk chicken wings in butter, one at a time. Dredge the wings in the parmesan cheese mixture and place on the baking sheet.
5. Bake the wings for about 40 – 60 minutes or until done.Cool for 5 minutes and serve.

Nutritional values per serving:

Calories – 348/Fat – 27 g/Carbohydrate – 1 g/Protein – 25 g

15.Simple Pan-Fried Chicken Breasts

Preparation time: 20 minutesCooking time: 5 – 8 minutesNumber of servings: 4 (8.7 oz each)

Ingredients:

- 8 chicken breast halves
- ½ teaspoon pepper or to taste
- 4 teaspoons grated parmesan cheese (optional)
- ½ teaspoon kosher salt or to taste
- ½ tablespoon olive oil

Directions:

1. To prepare the chicken: Place a sheet of plastic wrap on your countertop and add chicken. Cover with another sheet of plastic wrap and pound with a meat mallet until the chicken is flattened uniformly.
2. Season the chicken with salt and pepper. Let it rest for 15–20 minutes.
3. Place a cast-iron skillet over high heat—place chicken in the skillet. Let it cook undisturbed for 2–3 minutes uncovered until golden brown and the fat is released. Flip sides and cook for another 2–3 minutes. Remove the pan from heat.
4. Sprinkle parmesan cheese on top if using. Set the oven to broil and preheat it.
5. Place the skillet in the oven and broil until the cheese melts. Serve hot.

Nutritional values per serving:
Calories – 331.6/Fat – 12.9 g/Carbohydrate – 0.7 g/Protein – 50.2 g

16. Crispy Chicken Thighs

Preparation time: 5 minutesCooking time: 40 minutesNumber of servings: 2 (3 thighs)

Ingredients:

- 6 chicken thighs, with skin-on
- 1 tablespoon salt
- 2 tablespoons avocado oil or olive oil
- Freshly ground pepper to taste
- Kosher salt to taste
- Garlic powder to taste
- Paprika to taste

Directions:

1. Prepare a baking sheet by lining it with parchment paper. Make sure that your oven is preheated to 450° F.
2. Season the chicken thighs with salt, pepper, and preferred spices. Place it on the baking sheet, in a single layer, without overlapping.
3. Trickle oil over the chicken.
4. Roast the chicken for about 40 minutes or until the skin is crisp.

Nutritional values per serving:

Calories – 713/Fat – 56 g/Carbohydrate – 0 g/Protein – 48 g

17. Carnivore Chicken Nuggets

Preparation time: 40 minutesCooking time: 20 minutesNumber of servings: 30 nuggets (3 per)

Ingredients:

Chicken

- ☐ 1 ½ pounds ground chicken
- ☐ ¼ teaspoon pink salt or more to taste
- ☐ 1 small egg
- ☐ ¼ teaspoon dried oregano
- ☐ 1 teaspoon paprika

- ☐ ¼ teaspoon pepper
- ☐ ¼ teaspoon garlic powder
- ☐ ¼ teaspoon red pepper flakes

Breading

- ☐ ½ cup grated parmesan cheese
- ☐ ½ cup ground pork rinds

Directions:

1. Prepare a baking sheet by lining with a sheet of parchment paper.
2. Make sure that your oven is preheated to 400° F.
3. Add cheese and pork rinds in a bowl and mix well.
4. Beat the egg in a bowl and mix the chicken, salt and all the spices in it.
5. Divide the mixture into 30 equal portions and shape like nuggets.
6. Coat the nuggets in the rind mixture and place it on the baking sheet.

7. Bake the nuggets in an oven for about 20 to 25 minutes or until it becomes crisp and golden brown.

Nutritional values per serving:

Calories – 225/Fat – 12 g/Carbohydrate – 4 g/Protein – 27 g

18.Smokey Bacon Meatballs

Preparation time: 15 minutesCooking time: 30 minutesNumber of servings: 4 (3 meatballs per)

Ingredients:

- 1 chicken breast or ½ pound ground chicken
- 1 small egg
- ½ tablespoon onion powder
- 2 tablespoons olive oil or avocado oil

- 4 slices bacon, cooked, crumbled
- 1 clove garlic, peeled
- 1 drop liquid smoke
- Salt to taste

Directions:

1. Add chicken, egg, onion powder, bacon and garlic in the food processor bowl and process well.
2. Divide the mixture into small portions and make meatballs out of it. Place them on a plate.
3. Place a pan over medium flame. Add oil and let it heat. Add a few of the meatballs and cook until brown all over, turning the meatballs occasionally.
4. Remove and place on a paper towel.
5. Cook the remaining meatballs in batches. Sprinkle salt on top and serve hot.

Nutritional values per serving:

Calories – 280/Fat – 25 g/Carbohydrate – 1 g/Protein – 13 g

19. Chicken Bacon Sauté

Preparation time: 10 minutesCooking time: 20 minutesNumber of servings: 4

Ingredients:

- ☐ 2 chicken breasts, diced
- ☐ 2 tablespoons garlic powder
- ☐ Salt to taste
- ☐ 2 slices bacon, diced
- ☐ 1 tablespoon Italian seasoning
- ☐ ½ tablespoon avocado oil

Directions:

1. Place a large pan over medium flame. Add bacon and chicken and cook thoroughly.
2. Add garlic powder, salt, and Italian seasoning and serve.

Nutritional values per serving:

Calories – 526 | Fat – 43 g | Carbohydrate – 3 g | Protein – 30 g

20.Pepperoni Meatballs

Preparation time: 10 minutesCooking time: 15 minutesNumber of servings: 8 (2 meatballs each)

Ingredients:

- 2 pounds ground chicken
- 1 teaspoon salt or to taste
- 2 eggs, beaten

- 1 teaspoon pepper or to taste
- ½ pound pepperoni slices, minced
- Hot sauce to taste (optional)

Directions:

1. Combine chicken, salt, eggs, pepper, and pepperoni in a bowl.
2. Prepare a baking sheet by lining it with parchment paper and preheat your oven to 350° F.
3. Make 16 balls out of the mixture and place them on the baking sheet.
4. Bake the meatballs for about 20-30 minutes or until brown and cooked through. Toss the balls twice while baking, so they cook well. Or you can even cook the balls in a skillet.

Nutritional values per serving:

Calories – 451 | Fat – 37 g | Carbohydrate – 0 g \ Protein – 27 g

21.Parmesan Crusted Chicken Thighs

Preparation time: 10 minutesCooking time: 40 minutesNumber of servings: 4

Ingredients:

- 4 chicken thighs
- ½ cup freshly grated parmesan cheese
- ¼ teaspoon dried thyme
- ¼ teaspoon salt or to taste

- ½ teaspoon garlic powder
- 2 tablespoons butter, melted
- ½ tablespoon chopped parsley
- ½ teaspoon paprika
- ¼ teaspoon pepper

Directions:

1. Prepare a baking dish by greasing it with butter—preheat the oven to 400° F.
2. Pour melted butter in a shallow bowl.
3. Place salt, spices, herbs and parmesan cheese in a bowl. Mix well.
4. First, dip a chicken thigh in the bowl of butter. Lift it out the chicken thighs and let excess butter drip. Next, dredge it in the parmesan mixture and place it in the baking dish.
5. Repeat the previous step and coat the remaining chicken thighs.
6. Bake for about 35 – 50 minutes, depending on the size of the thighs. Serve hot.

Nutritional values per serving:

Calories – 401 | Fat – 32 g | Carbohydrate – 1 g | Protein – 24 g

22.Garlic Butter Chicken

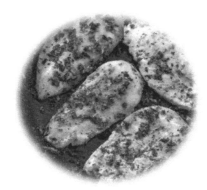

Preparation time: 5 minutesCooking time: 15 minutesNumber of servings: 8

Ingredients:

- 4 medium chicken breasts, cut into 2 halves horizontally (8 pieces in all)
- 2 teaspoons Italian seasoning
- Crushed chili pepper flakes to taste
- 8 cloves garlic, peeled, minced

- 2 tablespoons olive oil
- Salt to taste
- 4 tablespoons butter
- Pepper to taste
- ¼ cup chopped cilantro or parsley leaves

Directions:

1. Combine Italian seasoning, crushed red pepper, salt, and pepper in a bowl.
2. Sprinkle this mixture all over the chicken pieces.
3. Place a large pan over medium-high flame. Add oil and wait for a couple of minutes for the oil to heat.
4. Place chicken pieces in the pan and cook for 3 – 4 minutes, the underside should be golden brown. Turn the chicken pieces over and cook for 3 – 4 minutes.
5. Take out the chicken from the pan and place on a plate.
6. Lower the heat to medium-low heat. Add butter, garlic, parsley, and more crushed red pepper flakes and mix well.

7. Add chicken after about 20 – 30 seconds. Spoon the butter sauce over the chicken and cook for a couple of minutes, until garlic turns light golden brown. Serve hot.

Nutritional values per serving:

Calories – 150 | Fat – 10 g | Carbohydrate – 1 g | Protein – 12 g

23.Garlic Bacon Wrapped Chicken Bites

Preparation time: 10 minutesCooking time: 30 minutesNumber of servings: 2

Ingredients:

- ½ large chicken breast, cut into bite-size pieces
- 1 ½ tablespoon garlic powder
- 4 – 5 slices bacon, cut into thirds

Directions:

1. Prepare a baking sheet by lining it with foil.
2. Make sure that your oven is preheated to 400° F.
3. Spread garlic powder on a plate.
4. Dredge the chicken pieces in garlic powder, one at a time, and wrap it in a bacon piece.
5. Place it on the baking sheet. Leave a gap between the bites.
6. Place the baking sheet in the oven and cake until bacon is crisp, about 25 – 30 minutes. Turn the bites halfway through baking.

Nutritional values per serving:

Calories – 230 | Fat – 13 g | Carbohydrate – 1 g | Protein – 22 g

24.Pinchos de Pollo (Kebabs)

Preparation time: 10 minutes + marinating timeCooking time: 10 minutesNumber of servings: 2

Ingredients:

- ☐ ½ tablespoon minced garlic
- ☐ ¼ teaspoon freshly ground pepper
- ☐ ½ tablespoon extra-virgin olive oil

- ☐ ¾ pound boneless, skinless chicken breast, cut into 1-inch pieces
- ☐ Juice of ½ lime
- ☐ ¼ teaspoon fine Himalayan salt

- ☐ 1 teaspoon minced fresh oregano or ½ teaspoon dried oregano

Directions:

1. You need skewers for this recipe. You can use any kind of skewers, but if you are using wooden or bamboo ones, make sure it is soaked in water for a minimum of 30 minutes prior to grilling.
2. To make the marinade: Add garlic, oregano, salt, pepper, lime juice, and oil into a bowl and mix well.
3. Take a glass container with a lid and place chicken in it. Drizzle the marinade over the chicken and mix well.
4. Cover the lid of the bowl and refrigerate for 2 - 8 hours.

5. Now take out the bowl from the refrigerator and fix the chicken onto skewers. Do not leave a wide gap between the chicken pieces. Keep close together.

6. Set up your grill and preheat it to medium heat, about 330° F. Set it for direct cooking.

7. Grease the grill grates if desired. Place the skewers on the grill and grill until well done.

8. Serve right away.

Nutritional values per serving:

Calories – 290 | Fat – 10 g | Carbohydrate – 3 g | Protein – 39 g

25.Carnivore Waffles

Preparation time: 15 minutesCooking time: 5 minutes per waffleNumber of servings: 4 (1 waffle)

Ingredients:

- 4 ounces ground chicken or ground turkey
- 5 eggs
- 2 tablespoons dry parmesan cheese
- 4 ounces ground beef

Directions:

1. Place beef and chicken in a saucepan and add about 1 – 1-½ cups of water.
2. Place the pot over medium-high heat and bring to a boil. Lower the heat a little and cook for 5-7 minutes. Transfer the meat into a colander. Let it cool for 10 minutes.
3. Transfer the slightly cooled meat into the food processor bowl. Also, add eggs and parmesan. Process until really smooth.
4. Preheat waffle iron. Grease and spread ¼ of the mixture on iron. Cook waffle like you would for 5-7 minutes or until cooked.
5. Remove the waffle and place on a plate. Cool for a few minutes and serve. Repeat steps and make the other waffles.

Nutritional values per serving:

Calories – 257 | Fat – 16 g | Carbohydrate – 1 g | Protein – 27 g

26. Carnivore French Fries

Preparation time: 15 minutes Cooking time: 22 – 25 minutes Number of servings: 2

Ingredients:

- 8 ounces cooked poultry
- 2 eggs
- 0.7-ounce pork rinds
- ½ teaspoon salt

Directions:

1. Prepare a baking dish by lining it with parchment paper. Use a large baking dish or 2 smaller ones.
2. Add meat, eggs, salt, and pork rinds into the food processor bowl. Process until well combined and very slightly chunky.
3. Spoon the mixture into a plastic bag. Snip off a corner with scissors.
4. Squeeze the mixture and pipe onto the prepared baking dish, of the size you prefer. Leave sufficient gaps between the fries. Now flatten each of the fries slightly or to the desired thickness. Bake the fries for around 20 minutes.
5. Set the oven to broil mode. Broil for a couple of minutes or crisp on top.
6. Divide into 2 plates and serve.

Nutritional values per serving:

Calories – 248 | Fat – 10 g | Carbohydrate – 0 g | Protein – 38 g

Preparation time: 2 hours and 20 minutesCooking time: 12 – 15 minutesNumber of servings: 2
(2 drumsticks each)

Ingredients:

- 4 chicken drumsticks
- 5 – 6 cloves garlic, peeled
- ½ tablespoon of sea salt
- ¾ cup olive oil
- Juice of ½ lemon
- ¼ teaspoon pepper

Directions:

1. Mix oil, lemon juice, garlic, and seasonings together in a blender.
2. Brush the chicken with this mixture and rub in well.
3. Add chicken and stir well. Refrigerate for 2 – 8 hours.
4. Grill chicken on a preheated grill for 6 – 8 minutes on each side.

Nutritional values per serving:

Calories – 660 | Fat – 56 g | Carbohydrate – 4 g | Protein – 36 g

28.Salmon and Cream Cheese Bites

Preparation time: 10 minutesCooking time: 10 minutesNumber of servings: 18

Ingredients:

- ☐ 3 medium eggs
- ☐ ¼ teaspoon salt or to taste
- ☐ ½ teaspoon dried dill
- ☐ 0.88 ounce fresh or smoked salmon, chopped

- ☐ ½ cup cream
- ☐ 0.88-ounce grated parmesan
- ☐ 0.88-ounce cream cheese, diced

Directions:

1. Grease 18 wells of a mini muffin pan with some fat.
2. Make sure that your oven is preheated to 360° F.
3. Add eggs into a bowl and whisk well. Add salt and cream and whisk well.
4. Add parmesan, cream cheese, and dill and stir.

5. Divide the egg mixture into the 18 wells of the mini muffin pan.

6. Drop at least 1 – 2 pieces of salmon in each well.

7. Place the mini muffin pan in the oven and bake for about 12 – 15 minutes or until set.

8. Cool the mini muffins on your countertop.

9. Remove them from the molds and serve.

Nutritional values per serving:

Calories – 44 | Fat – 4 g | Carbohydrate – 0.1 g | Protein – 1 g

29.Baked Fish Fillets

Preparation time: 5 minutesCooking time: 20 minutesNumber of servings: 3

Ingredients:

- 2 tablespoons butter, melted
- A pinch ground paprika
- 3 fish fillets (5 ounces)
- Pepper to taste
- 1 tablespoon lemon juice
- ½ teaspoon salt

Directions:

1. Make sure that your oven is preheated to 350° F.
2. Prepare a baking pan by greasing it with some fat.
3. Sprinkle salt and pepper over the fillets and place them in the pan.
4. Add butter, paprika, and lemon juice into a bowl and stir. Brush this mixture over the fillets.
5. Place the baking pan in the oven and bake the fillets for 15-25 minutes, until the fish flakes easily when pierced with a fork.

Nutritional values per serving:

Calories – 399 | Fat – 31 g | Carbohydrate – 0.5 g | Protein – 28.3 g

30.Salmon Cakes

Preparation time: 10 minutesCooking time: 10 minutesNumber of servings: 8

Ingredients:

- 2 cans salmon (14.75 ounces each), drained
- 8 tablespoons collagen
- 2 cups shredded mozzarella cheese
- 1 teaspoon onion powder
- 4 large pastured eggs
- 4 teaspoons dried dill
- 1 teaspoon pink sea salt or to taste
- 4 tablespoons bacon grease

Directions:

1. Add salmon, collagen, mozzarella, onion powder, eggs, dill, and salt into a bowl and mix well.
2. Make 8 patties from the mixture.
3. Place a large skillet over a medium-low flame with bacon grease. Once the fat is well heated, place the salmon cakes in the skillet and cook until it becomes golden brown on all sides.
4. Take off the pan from heat and let the patties remain in the cooked fat for 5 minutes.Serve.

Nutritional values per serving:

Calories – 357 | Fat – 21 g | Carbohydrate – 1 g | Protein – 40 g

31. Grilled Split Lobster

Preparation time: 10 minutes **Cooking time:** 12 – 15 minutes **Number of servings:** 4

Ingredients:

- 4 tablespoons olive oil or melted butter
- Kosher salt to taste
- 4 live lobsters (1 ½ pound each)
-

- Freshly ground pepper to taste
- Melted butter to serve

- Hot sauce like Frank's hot sauce, to serve
- Lemon wedges to serve

Directions:

1. Place the live lobsters in the freezer for 15 minutes.
2. Place them on your cutting board with the belly down on the cutting board. Hold the tail. Split the lobsters in half lengthwise. Start from the point where the tail joins the body and go up to the head. Flip sides and cut it lengthwise via the tail.
3. Rub melted butter on the cut part, immediately after cutting it. Sprinkle salt and pepper over it.

4. Set up your grill and preheat it to high heat for 5-10 minutes. Clean the grill grate and lower the heat to low heat.

5. Place the lobsters on the grill and press the claws on the grill until cooked—grill for 6-8 minutes.

6. Flip sides and cook until it is cooked through and lightly charred.

7. Transfer on to a plate. Drizzle melted butter on top and serve.

Nutritional values per serving:

Calories – 290 | Fat – 16 g | Carbohydrate – 0 g | Protein – 36 g

32.Fish Bone Broth

Preparation time: 5 minutesCooking time: 4 hoursNumber of servings: 8

Ingredients:

- 2 pounds of fish head or carcass
- Salt to taste
- 7 – 8 quarts water + extra to blanch
- 2 inches ginger, sliced
- 2 tablespoons lemon juice

Directions:

1. To blanch the fish: Add water and fish heads into a large pot. Place the pot over high heat.
2. When it boils, turn the heat off and discard the water.
3. Place the fish back in the pot. Pour 7–8 quarts of water.
4. Place the pot over high heat. Add ginger, salt, and lemon juice.
5. When the mixture boils, reduce the heat and cover with a lid. Simmer for 4 hours.
6. Remove from heat. When it cools down, strain into a large jar with a wire mesh strainer.
7. Refrigerate for 5–6 days. Unused broth can be frozen.

Nutritional values per serving:

Calories – 40 | Fat – 2 g | Carbohydrate – 0 g | Protein – 5 g

33. Garlic Butter Shrimp

Preparation time: 10 minutes Cooking time: 10 minutes Number of servings: 8 (4 shrimp per)

Ingredients:

- 1 cup unsalted butter, divided
- Kosher salt to taste
- ½ cup chicken stock
- Freshly ground pepper to taste
- ¼ cup chopped fresh parsley leaves
- 3 pounds medium shrimp, peeled, deveined
- 10 cloves garlic, peeled, minced
- Juice of 2 lemons

Directions:

1. Add 4 tablespoons butter into a large skillet and place the skillet over medium-high flame. Once butter melts, stir in salt, shrimp, and pepper and cook for 2 – 3 minutes. Stir every minute or so. Remove shrimp with a slotted spoon and place on a plate.

2. Add garlic into the pot and cook until you get a nice aroma. Pour lemon juice and stock and stir.

3. Once it comes to a boil, lower the heat and cook until the stock reduces to half its initial quantity.

4. Add rest of the butter, a tablespoon each time, and stir until it melts each time.

5. Add shrimp and stir lightly until well coated.

6. Sprinkle parsley on top and serve.

Nutritional values per serving:

Calories – 209.7 | Fat – 23.3 g | Carbohydrate – 2.6 g | Protein – 15.5 g

34. Grilled Shrimp

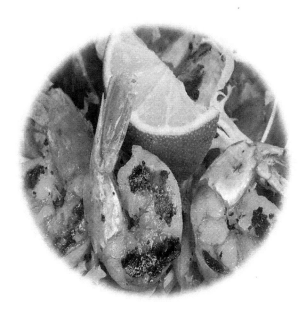

Preparation time: 10 minutesCooking time: 5 minutesNumber of servings: 8

Ingredients:

Shrimp Seasoning

- 2 teaspoons garlic powder
- 2 teaspoons Italian seasoning
- 2 teaspoons kosher salt
- ½ – 1 teaspoon cayenne pepper

Grilling

- 4 tablespoons extra-virgin olive oil
- 2 pounds shrimp, peeled, deveined
- 2 tablespoons fresh lemon juice
- Oil to grease the grill grated

Directions:

1. You can grill the shrimp in a grill or boil it in an oven. Choose whatever method suits you and preheat the grill or oven to high heat.
2. In case you are broiling it in an oven, prepare a baking sheet by lining it with foil and greasing the foil as well, with some fat.
3. Add garlic powder, cayenne pepper, salt and Italian seasoning into a large bowl and mix well.
4. Add lemon juice and oil and mix well.

5. Stir in the shrimp. Make sure that the shrimp are well coated with the mixture.

6. If using the grill, fix the shrimp on skewers else place them on the baking sheet.

7. Grease the grill grates with some oil. Grill the shrimp or broil them in an oven until they turn pink. It should take 2 – 3 minutes for each side.

Nutritional values per serving:

Calories – 102 | Fat – 3 g | Carbohydrate – 1 g | Protein – 28 g

35.Garlic Ghee Pan-Fried Cod

Preparation time: 5 minutesCooking time: 10 minutesNumber of servings: 2

Ingredients:

- 2 cod fillets (4.8 ounces each)
- 3 cloves garlic, peeled, minced
- Salt to taste
- 1 ½ tablespoons ghee
- ½ tablespoon garlic powder (optional)

Directions:

1. Place a pan over medium-high flame. Add ghee.
2. Once ghee melts, stir in half the garlic and cook for about 6 – 10 seconds.
3. Add fillets and season with garlic powder and salt.
4. Soon the color of fish will turn absolutely white. This color should be visible for about half the height of the fish.
5. Turn the fish over and cook, adding remaining garlic.
6. When the entire fillet turns white, remove from the pan, and serve.

Nutritional values per serving:

Calories – 160 | Fat – 7 g | Carbohydrate – 1 g | Protein – 21 g

36.Pan-Seared Beef Tongue

Preparation time: 5 minutesCooking time: 40 minutesNumber of servings: 2 (4 ounces each)

Ingredients:

- 2 whole beef tongues, rinsed
- 2 tablespoons lard or butter
- 6 cups of water
- Seasoning of your choice

Directions:

1. It is best to cook it in an instant pot or pressure cooker.
2. Add water and tongues into an instant pot and cook on 'Manual' for 35 minutes. Let the pressure release naturally.
3. If you do not have an instant pot, pour water into a saucepan. Add tongues and place saucepan over medium heat.
4. When it begins to boil, lower the heat to low heat. Cook covered until tender.
5. Remove tongues and place them on your cutting board. When cool enough to handle, cut into slices. Sprinkle the seasoning of your choice over it.

6. Place a pan over medium flame. Add butter. Once butter melts, place tongue slices in the pan and sear for 2-3 minutes. Once done on one end, cook the other side until you get a good golden-brown color. Serve hot.

Nutritional values per serving:

Calories – 447.87 | Fat – 39.27 g | Carbohydrate – 0 g | Protein – 21.86 g

Preparation time: 10 minutes + marinatingCooking time: 10 minutesNumber of servings: 8

Ingredients:

- 8 ounces kidney fat, optional but advisable, cut into cubes
- 2.2 pounds fresh calf or lamb liver (preferably calf liver), remove the transparent membrane, cut into ¾ inch cubes

Marinade

- 2 tablespoons ground sweet paprika
- 2 teaspoons salt
- 1 teaspoon ground cumin

To serve

- 2 teaspoons ground cumin
- 2 teaspoons cayenne pepper (optional)
- 2 teaspoons salt

Directions:

1. Place liver and fat in a bowl and toss well.
2. Sprinkle paprika, salt, and cumin over it and toss once again until well coated.
3. Cover the bowl and refrigerate for 1 – 8 hours.
4. 30 minutes before grilling, remove the bowl from the refrigerator.
5. Set up your grill and preheat it to medium-high heat.

6. Fix the liver cubes alternately with kidney fat cubes onto skewers, without leaving any gap in between. Place about 6 – 8 cubes of liver on each skewer.

7. Place the prepared skewers on the grill and grill for about 8 – 10 minutes, turning frequently. The liver should be cooked well inside and spongy when you press it.

8. Serve hot.

Nutritional values per serving:

Calories – 355 | Fat – 9 g | Carbohydrate – 12 g | Protein – 51 g

38.Carnivore Quiche (Organ Meat Pie)

Preparation time: 5 minutesCooking time: 15 minutesNumber of servings: 8

Ingredients:

- 1-pound ground beef
- 1-pound ground beef liver
- 1-pound ground beef heart
- Butter or ghee or beef tallow or any other animal fat of
- your choice, to cook, as required
- Salt to taste
- 6 eggs

Directions:

1. Take 2 pie plates (9 inches) and grease them lightly with some butter or ghee.
2. Make sure that your oven is preheated to 360° F.
3. Add beef, beef liver, beef heart, salt, and eggs into a bowl and mix well.
4. Divide the mixture into the 2 pie plates.
5. Bake the meat pies until set, around 15 to 20 minutes.
6. Cut each into 4 equal wedges when done and serve.

Nutritional values per serving:

Calories – 412 | Fat – 28 g | Carbohydrate – 2 g | Protein – 35 g

39.Easy Beef Heart

Preparation time: 5 minutesCooking time: 20 minutesNumber of servings: 2 (1 ball each)

Ingredients:

- 4 ounces ground beef heart
- 4 ounces ground beef
- ½ teaspoon salt

Directions:

1. Add a ground beef heart, ground beef, and salt into a bowl and mix well.
2. Divide the mixture into 2 portions and make balls.
3. Keep them in a baking dish made of glass.
4. Make sure that your oven is preheated to 360° F.
5. Place the baking dish in the oven and bake until meat is well cooked inside about 20 minutes.

Nutritional values per serving:

Calories – 208 | Fat – 14 g | Carbohydrate – 1 g | Protein – 20 g

40. Carnivore Cake

Preparation time: 15 minutesCooking time: 2 hours and 30 minutesNumber of servings: 6

Ingredients:

Braunschweiger

- ¼ pound pork shoulder or beef tongue, cut into cubes
- 10 ounces pork or beef liver, cut into cubes
- 2 hard-boiled eggs, peeled

- 6 ounces pork back fat, cut into cubes
- 1 ½ teaspoon pink sea salt

For topping

- 6 slices prosciutto or Carpaccio
- 6 slices bacon

Directions:

1. Make this dish 1 to 2 days before eating.
2. Add pork liver, shoulder, and fat cubes in a food processor and process well.
3. Pour it into a springform pan. Cover the pan with foil such that water does not enter into the pan. Make sure that it is tightly wrapped.
4. Take a roasting pan, larger than the springform pan and pour an inch of boiling water at the bottom of the pan.
5. Place the springform pan in the roasting pan.

6. Place the roasting pan along with the springform pan in the oven for about 2 hours. Make sure that your oven preheated to 300° F before placing the roasting pan in the oven.
7. Take out the springform pan from the oven. Make 2 wells in the pan, big enough for an egg to fit in. Place a boiled egg in each well. Cover the eggs with a spoonful of meat.
8. Cool and place in the refrigerator for 1 – 2 days.
9. Place prosciutto and bacon slices on top. Serve.

Nutritional values per serving:

Calories – 409 | Fat – 34 g | Carbohydrate – 2 g | Protein – 24 g

41.Easy Beef Kidney Bites

Preparation time: 6 minutesCooking time: 8 minutesNumber of servings: 8 (4 oz each)

Ingredients:

- 2 beef kidneys
- Cold butter to serve (optional)
- Salt to taste (optional)

Directions:

1. Place kidneys in a pot and cover with water.

2. Place the pot over medium-high flame.

3. Once it begins to boil, simmer on medium-low heat, partially covered.

4. Drain off the water after 8 minutes.

5. If you prefer, you can rinse the kidney in water.

6. Cut into bite-size pieces. Season with salt and serve with butter if using.

Nutritional values per serving:

Calories – 170 | Fat – 4 g | Carbohydrate – 1 g | Protein – 20 g

42.Beef and Chicken Liver Burgers

Preparation time: 10 minutesCooking time: 15 minutesNumber of servings: 2

Ingredients:

- 2 ounces of chicken liver
- 10 grass-fed beef
- ½ teaspoon poultry seasoning

- ½ teaspoon salt
- ¾ teaspoon ground coriander
- ½ teaspoon pepper

Directions:

1. Add chicken liver, beef, poultry seasoning, salt, coriander, and pepper in a food processor and process well.
2. Make 2 patties from the mixture
3. Preheat the grill to medium-high heat.
4. Grill the burgers on both sides as your preference.
5. Serve hot.

Nutritional values per serving:

Calories – 396 | Fat – 11 g | Carbohydrate – 1 g | Protein – 29 g

43.Chicken Hearts

Preparation time: 5 minutesCooking time: 30 minutesNumber of servings: 6 (5.3 ounces per)

Ingredients:

- 2 pounds chicken hearts, pat dried with paper towels
- 2 teaspoons cayenne pepper or to taste
- 2 teaspoons pepper or to taste

- 2 teaspoons salt or to taste
- 2 teaspoons garlic powder
- 2 teaspoons onion powder or to taste
- Frank's hot sauce to serve

Directions:

1. Prepare a baking dish by lining it with foil.
2. Place the chicken hearts in the baking dish. Sprinkle the spices and toss well.
3. Make sure that your oven is preheated to 350° F.
4. Bake the chicken hearts for about 30 minutes.
5. Serve hot.

Nutritional values per serving:

Calories – 239 | Fat – 14 g | Carbohydrate – 3 g | Protein – 24 g

44.Roasted Bone Marrow

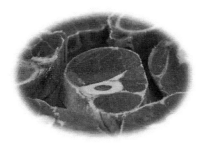

Preparation time: 5 minutesCooking time: 30 minutesNumber of servings: 4 (2 halves each)

Ingredients:

- ☐ 8 bone marrow halves
- ☐ 1 tablespoon chopped parsley, to garnish

- ☐ Freshly ground pepper to taste
- ☐ Sea salt flakes

Directions:

1. Place the bone marrow halves with the marrow facing up on a rimmed baking dish.
2. Make sure that your oven is preheated to 350° F.
3. Bake the marrows for about 20 – 25 minutes until marrow is crisp and golden brown.
4. Sprinkle salt and parsley on top and serve.

Nutritional values per serving:

Calories – 440 | Fat – 48 g | Carbohydrate – 0 g | Protein – 4 g

45.Chicken Liver Pate

Preparation time: 10 minutesCooking time: 5 minutesNumber of servings: 3

Ingredients:

- 4 ounces chicken livers, trimmed, discard sinew
- ½ teaspoon onion powder
- ½ tablespoon minced parsley
- Pepper to taste
- ¼ cup butter or duck fat
- 1 clove garlic, peeled, minced
- ¼ teaspoon salt

Directions:

1. Place a skillet with ½ tablespoon butter over medium flame. When butter melts, add garlic and stir for 30 – 45 seconds until aromatic.
2. Add liver and cook until golden brown all over.
3. Add parsley and mix well. Turn off the heat after a minute.
4. Cool for a while and transfer into a food processor bowl. Also, add the rest of the butter and salt and process until well pureed.
5. Spoon into 3 ramekins. Cover with cling wrap and refrigerate for 4 – 8 hours.Serve chilled.

Nutritional values per serving:

Calories – 185 | Fat – 17 g | Carbohydrate – 1 g | Protein – 7 g

Conclusion

Thank you once again for choosing *The Carnivore Diet Cookbook.* I hope you enjoyed the recipes and found them useful.

The carnivore diet is a straightforward protocol and is entirely a meat-based diet. This diet includes all types of animal-based foods, eggs, and dairy products in limited quantities. This isn't a new concept, and it's believed to be the natural way of life, followed by our cavemen ancestors. By following this diet, you can obtain all the different benefits it offers. From stabilizing your blood sugar levels to increasing your muscle growth, enhancing your energy levels, and getting all the different nutrients your body needs, there is a lot to obtain from the carnivore diet. Irrespective of whether it's your overall health or weight loss goals, you can achieve them all with this diet.

In this book, you were given several easy to cook carnivore diet-based recipes. You were also provided a simple two-week meal plan to get you accustomed to this diet. You don't have to cook for hours to cook healthy and nutritious meals. Once you start following this diet, you will realize how simple it is. All you need to do is get the right ingredients, choose a recipe and get started.

Good luck and all the best on your meat-eating journey!

Manufactured by Amazon.ca
Bolton, ON

30281941R00046